To:

_____

From:

_____

Date:

_____

Loving Thoughts for Mom

© 2013 Christian Art Gifts, RSA
       Christian Art Gifts Inc., IL, USA

Designed by Christian Art Gifts

Images used under license from Shutterstock.com

Scripture quotations are taken from the Holy Bible, New International Version®
NIV®. Copyright © 1973, 1978, 1984 by International Bible Society.
Used by permission of Zondervan Publishing House. All rights reserved.

Printed in China

ISBN 978-1-4321-0459-7

Loving Thoughts for Mom

christian
art gifts®

A mother holds her
children's hands for a while …
their hearts forever.

Anonymous

The LORD is good.
His *unfailing love*
continues forever,
and His *faithfulness*
continues to each generation.

Ps. 100:5

The Lord will work out His plans for my life – for Your faithful love, O Lord, endures forever.

Ps. 138:8

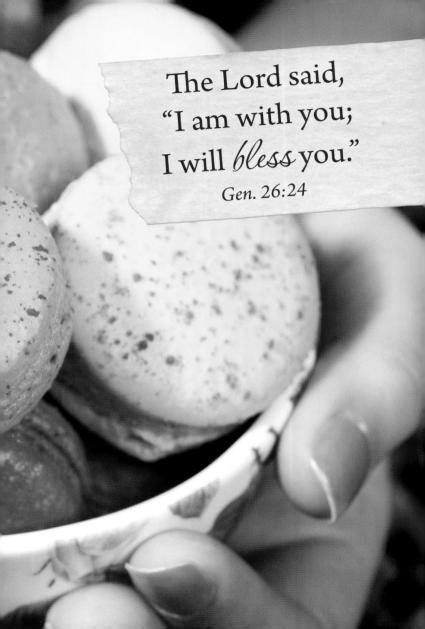

The Lord said,
"I am with you;
I will *bless* you."

Gen. 26:24

Those who *hope*
in the LORD
will *renew* their strength.
They will *soar* on wings
like eagles;
they will *run*
and not grow weary,
they will *walk*
and not be faint.

Isa. 40:31

May the LORD *bless* you and *protect* you. May the LORD *smile* on you and be *gracious* to you. May the LORD show you His *favor* and give you His *peace*.

Num. 6:24-26

Who can ever measure the benefit of a mother's inspiration? Charles R. Swindoll

God's way is perfect. All the LORD's promises prove true, Ps. 18:30

When the stresses and strains
of everyday life feel overwhelming,
hug your child.
You will be embracing all
that is good in the world.

Anonymous

A mother's hand brushes
hair from your eyes,
tears from your cheek,
hurt from your heart.

Lauren Benson

The best medicine in the
world is a mother's kiss.

Anonymous

He will cover you with His feathers. He will shelter you with His wings. His faithful promises are your armor and protection. *Ps. 91:4*

"Be still, and know that I am God!"

Ps. 46:10

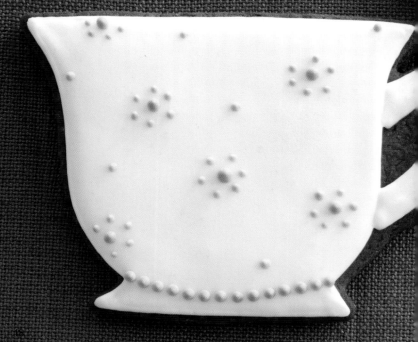

We *praise* God for the glorious grace
He has poured out on us.

Eph. 1:6

Youth fades; love droops;
the leaves of friendship fall;
a mother's secret hope
outlives them all.

Oliver Wendell Holmes

Though distance
may come between
a mother and her
child, the bond that
holds them close
will never weaken –
the love they
share will never be
more than a
memory apart.

Dean Walley

Love

never gives up,

never loses faith,

is always hopeful,

and endures through

every circumstance.

1 Cor. 13:7

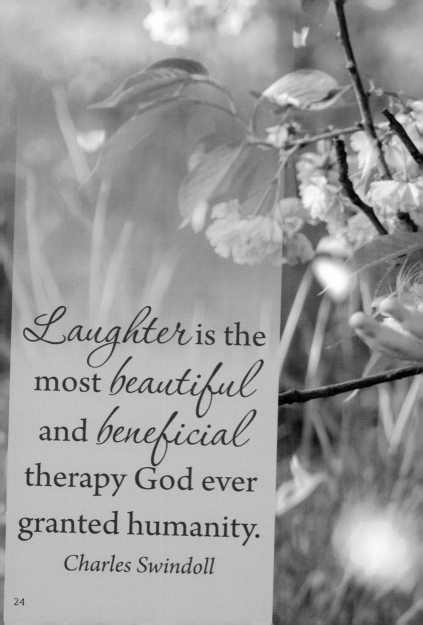

Laughter is the most *beautiful* and *beneficial* therapy God ever granted humanity.

Charles Swindoll

The loveliest masterpiece of the heart of God is the heart of a mother.

~ Saint Thérèse of Lisieux ~

Mother means
selfless devotion,
limitless sacrifice,
and *love* that
passes understanding.

Anonymous

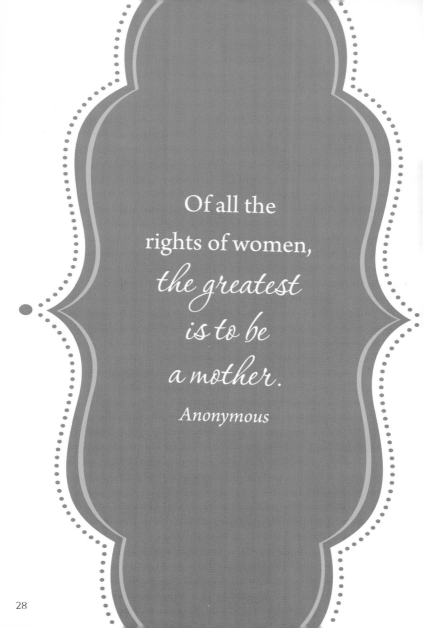

Of all the
rights of women,
*the greatest
is to be
a mother.*

Anonymous

A mother understands
what a child does not say.

Jewish Proverb

Every time you
smile at someone,

it is an act of love,

a gift to that person,

a *beautiful* thing.

Mother Teresa

A mother seems to *understand* the things
that can't be said;
she looks beyond our words
and reads our hearts instead.
A mother *shows the love*
she knows with tenderness
anew; when God gave
me a mother I'm glad
that it was *you*.

Anne Peterson

Keep the joy of loving
God in your heart and
share this joy with all you
meet, especially your family.

Mother Teresa

Nothing can ever Separate us from God's Love.

Rom. 8:38

All glory to Jesus,
my loving King,
He *blesses* me every day.

James D. Vaughan

May the Almighty bless
you with the blessings
of the heavens above.
Gen. 49:25

Mother love is the fuel that
enables a normal human being
to do the impossible.
Marion C. Garretty

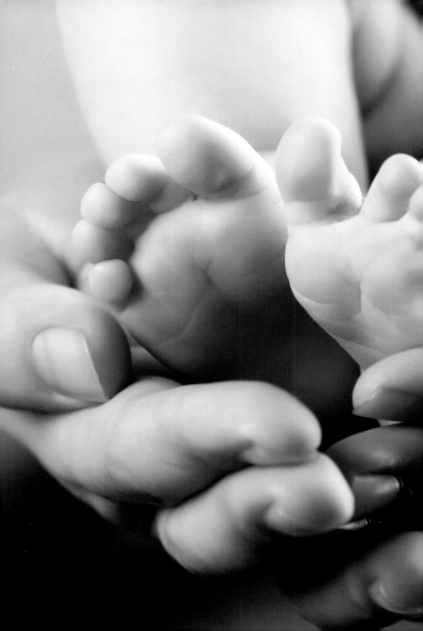

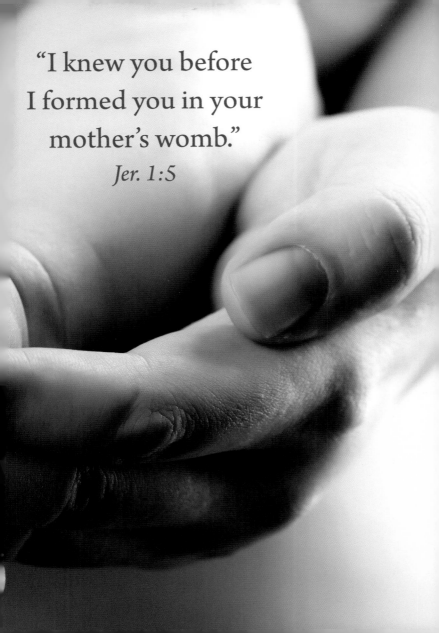

"I knew you before
I formed you in your
mother's womb."

Jer. 1:5

MOM is WOW UPSIDE DOWN.

Anonymous

From His
abundance
we have all
received one
gracious
blessing
after another.

John 1:16

A mother's love is a glimpse of heaven.

Joseph E. Beck